The Spirit of Jesus in
ACTS

The Spirit of Jesus in
ACTS

Paul Siebert, O.M.I.

Ave Maria Press~Notre Dame, Indiana 46556

Paul Siebert, O.M.I., resides at the Oblate Education Centre, Hurstville (Sydney), Australia, a center specializing in vocational counseling, community work, retreats and religious education.

Nihil Obstat:
    David Burrell, C.S.C.
    Censor Deputatus

Imprimatur:
    William E. McManus, D.D.
    Bishop of Fort Wayne-South Bend

© 1980 by Ave Maria Press, Notre Dame, Indiana 46556
All rights reserved.

Originally published in serial form by the Oblate Community, Hurstville, N.S.W. 2220, Australia.

Library of Congress Catalog Card Number: 80-67318
International Standard Book Number: 0-87793-207-7

Cover design: Joyce Stanley DePalma

Manufactured in the United States of America.

Table of Contents

The Purpose of This Program 7
1. Kerygma 9
2. The Gift of the Spirit 15
3. Community in the Spirit 21
4. Mission 27
5. Salvation for Pagans 33
6. Paul 39
7. To Europe 45
8. To Rome in Chains 51
Map 1 57
Map 2 59
Map 3 61
Map 4 63

The Purpose of This Program

a. Very simply it is that you may have *life*—joy, meaning, vision, purpose, direction—and have it to the full.

b. It is to help you understand the role of the Spirit of Jesus in the Church, and to lead you to yield to his action in your life.

c. It is that you may get an introduction to or a fuller appreciation of the *word of God in the Bible* and so be encouraged to read and pray it more.

d. It is that you may learn for the first time or grow in the experience of *praying over God's word* in the scriptures.

e. It is to help you *grow in faith* with a group of fellow Christians as you experience Jesus' promise together—"For where two or three are gathered in my name, I am there with them."

NOTE: Although these pages are based on sound and up-to-date biblical scholarship, they are *not* a study course, but rather a small effort to help you grow in faith and in love of God.

Private Use

Using the pages alone, while not ideal, will certainly help you.

Here are a few suggestions:

a. Set apart a definite time to read slowly through the thoughts on each page and the texts to which the pages refer you.

b. Stop as the Lord moves you to ponder and pray while you do this. It is not a matter of getting it done but more a matter of meeting God in a friendly, relaxed and unhurried manner.

c. The Points to Ponder and the Points to Pray can be used also for the purpose of helping you gain more out of your encounter with God.

In a Group (10 would be a maximum)

This is the ideal way to go through the pages and through the texts of the Gospel. It consists of small prayer meetings, each one planned ahead at the end of the previous one.

Here are a few suggestions:

a. It is essential that, as above, time be given *before* each meeting to reading and praying over the pages and the gospel texts alone.

b. Points to Share are added for the meetings, but any point may be used as the Lord leads.

c. Genuine sharing must take place and care taken to *avoid* discussion and debate.

d. Give each person as much time as he or she needs while sharing and praying in turn.

e. A period of silence for personal reflection and prayer is important after each one has finished sharing.

1
Kerygma

"Seeing that many others have undertaken to draw up accounts of the events that have taken place among us, exactly as these were handed down to us by those who from the outset were eye-witnesses and ministers of the word, I in my turn, after carefully going over the whole story from the beginning, have decided to write an ordered account for you, Theophilus, so that your Excellency may learn how well founded the teaching is that you have received" (Lk 1:1-4).

This introduction to Luke's Gospel is probably the prologue to his entire work of two volumes: the Gospel and the Acts of the Apostles. Not long after the publication of John's Gospel, around the beginning of the second century, the four Gospels were gathered together in one collection and began to circulate as the fourfold Gospel. This caused the separation of Luke's two volumes, and the Acts of the Apostles was left on its own, especially when the Epistles of Paul were made into a second collection.

Important Link

Acts provides the sequel to the Gospels and the narrative background against which the Epistles of Paul can readily be understood. In the middle of the second century in Rome, Marcion taught that Christ was the revealer of a completely new religion, which had no connection with the Old Testament. The Acts of the Apostles became the main proof to refute his claims, and was placed between the Gospels and the Epistles: a place it occupies to this day. Luke is the only non-Jewish (Gentile) author of a book of the New Testament, and he is described by St. Paul as "my dear friend Luke, the doctor" (Col 4:14). He depicts the emergence of Christianity from its Jewish matrix into a religion of worldwide status, and traces the action of the Spirit as the power making this possible. He dedicates his second volume, as he did his first, to someone called Theophilus (meaning God-lover).

Read and pray over chapter 1:1-5.

Apologetic Emphasis

The Roman Empire, in which Christianity started off, was very concerned with law and order. Jesus was executed by the sentence of the procurator Pontius Pilate on a charge of sedition, and wherever it spread, Christianity seemed to cause tumult and disorder. Luke sets himself to show that the crucifixion of Christ was a gross miscarriage of justice. Pilate had pronounced him not guilty of the charges of sedition, and Herod Antipas agreed that there was no substance in the charges. Romans, both government officials and soldiers, are presented in a favorable light (13:12, 18:12-16, 16:35, 19:31) while the Pharisees, scribes and Jewish leaders are the cause of all the strife and disorder. Christians are good and loyal citizens.

Read and pray over chapter 14:5-7 and 19-20.

Role of the Spirit

The Holy Spirit, promised by Jesus and given at Pentecost, is mentioned over 40 times in Acts, and there is great emphasis on the role of the Spirit in the church. The community is spirit-filled (5:3 and 15:28) and spirit-led (16:6), and the whole evangelistic enterprise from Jerusalem to Rome is directed by the Spirit.

Over one-third of Acts is made up of discourses or speeches. Mostly they are a literary device composed by Luke and put into the mouths of his heroes. The Spirit inspired his use of this way of presenting an account of the proclamation of the Good News in Jerusalem, Judea, Samaria, Asia Minor, Europe, and finally in Rome.

Speeches

Peter to the Jews: Chapters 2:14-39 at Pentecost; 3:11-26 in the Temple; 4:8-12 before the Sanhedrin; 5:29-32 before the Sanhedrin.

Peter to the Pagans: Chapter 10:34-43 in Caesarea.

Stephen to the Jews: Chapter 7:2-53 before the Sanhedrin.

Paul: Chapters 13:16-41 at Pisidian Antioch to the Jews; 17:22-31 at Athens to Greek pagans; 20:18-35 at Ephesus to Christian elders; 22:3-21 at Jerusalem to a Jewish mob; 24:10-21 at Caesarea before Governor Felix; 26:1-23 at Caesarea before King Agrippa; 28:17-29 at Rome to Jewish leaders.

There will be opportunity to read these discourses in context later, but we suggest that you read prayerfully one of Peter's and one of Paul's NOW, so as to grasp the sense of their preaching. Paul's speech at Athens (17:22-31) is one of the earliest examples of Christian apologetic to the pagans. Stephen's speech (7:2-53) is a prototype of Christian apologetic against the Jews, designed to demonstrate that Christianity and not

Judaism is the true fulfillment of the revelation given through Moses and the prophets. Peter's speech at Pentecost (2:14-39) is a fine example of early apostolic kerygma. It falls into four parts:

I. The last days are here, the age of fulfillment has arrived.
II. An account of the ministry, death, and triumph of Jesus.
III. Quotes from the Old Testament prophecies whose fulfillment proves Jesus to be the Messiah.
IV. A call to repentance.

Repentance *(Metanoia)*

Our use of the word "repentance" in English suggests a merely negative aspect associated with regret for sins. This is part of it, of course, but only in function of the broader and deeper significance of a changing heart embracing the entire revelation of God in Christ. John the Baptist preached a turning from sins and an opening of the mind in the right direction to prepare for the coming of the Lord. His teaching was incomplete and ineffective in bringing about a definitive change of heart. Positive acceptance of Christ brings about the promises of God in his self-revelation and salvation of man. Turn from selfishness and sinfulness, and turn to Jesus as Lord and Savior—this is the message of the apostolic preaching. To accept Christ as Savior is to be in the kingdom and to be saved. Let us now look at this theme of repentance as it was preached by the apostles.

Read and pray over chapters 2:38; 3:19 and 26; 5:31; 10:43; 11:18; 13:24; 17:30; 19:4; 20:21; 26:20.

The believer must surrender his whole life to the rule of Jesus, and his repentance must embrace all of God's revelation. He must turn from sins, turn to Christ, accept forgiveness of sins and receive the Holy

Spirit—Paul expressed this beautifully to the Philippians: "Nothing can happen that will outweigh the supreme advantage of knowing Christ Jesus my Lord. I am no longer trying for perfection by my own efforts, the perfection that comes from the Law, but I want only the perfection that comes through faith in Christ, and is from God and based on faith." This new life is a free gift from God to anyone who will turn to him for it, and hear him saying in Jesus, "I have forgiven you." It is not a matter of doing things by my own efforts in obeying God's Law so that he will love me; but rather of believing in his love for me and accepting his free gift to be able to live his kind of life. Our recent past has been more concerned with the things we were turning from (sins and selfishness) than with the One to whom we must turn in expectant faith for the power to be able to renounce sin. Peter said, "Now you must repent and turn to God, so that your sins may be wiped out" (Acts 3:19). St. Paul could say to the Corinthians, "I shall be very happy to make my weaknesses my special boast so that the power of Christ may stay over me" (2 Cor 12:9). The Jews must turn from their distorted view of the kingdom, and the pagans from their ignorance to the One True God.

THOSE WHO REPENT AND TURN TO GOD FOR
FORGIVENESS OF THEIR SINS
WILL RECEIVE THE HOLY SPIRIT

Points to Ponder Alone:

1. Am I an Old Testament person trying to live a New Testament life by willpower and observance of laws, or do I experience grace enabling me to change?

2. Am I more preoccupied with the sins I am trying to turn from, than with the love and power of the Savior to whom I turn for help?

Points to Pray Privately:
1. The church expresses its message in the terms which its present self-consciousness suggests. In what way do you hear the church calling you to repentance today, and to what aspect of Jesus do you hear yourself called to turn?
2. Thank God for his free gift of salvation in Jesus.
3. Recognize that in this life there will always need to be a conversion from sinfulness as well as a new experience of spiritual success in the power of the Spirit of Jesus.

Points to Share with the Group:
1. Share what the scriptures have said to you about the life of a Christian.
2. Share what "to turn from sin and to turn to God" means for you in the repentance theme.
3. What most impressed you about the kerygma preached by the apostles?

2
The Gift of the Spirit

Just prior to his ascension Jesus instructed his apostles: "He opened their minds to understand the scriptures. He said to them, 'So you see how it is written that the Christ would suffer and on the third day rise from the dead and that, in his name, repentance for the forgiveness of sins would be preached to all the nations, beginning from Jerusalem. And now I am sending down to you what the Father has promised. Stay in the city then, until you are clothed with power from on high'" (Lk 24:45-49). He had explained this promise of the Father to them as he was at table with them after the Last Supper:

"I shall ask the Father, and he will give you another Advocate (besides me) to be with you forever" (Jn 14:16). *"He will teach you everything and remind you of all I have said to you"* (Jn 14:26). *"He will lead you to the complete truth . . . He will glorify me"* (Jn 16:13-14).

By the power of this Spirit those who believe in Jesus become members of his Body. When the Holy Spirit came upon Mary and the power of the Most High covered her with its shadow, the Son of God became man; the Incarnation was an established fact (Lk 1:35). While Jesus was at prayer, after his baptism in the river Jordan by John the Baptist, heaven opened and the Holy Spirit descended on him in bodily shape, like a dove. Jesus was anointed by the Spirit as the Christ, as Messiah, as Savior. He was constituted or established in that role by this reception of the Holy Spirit (Lk 3:21-22).

The church is the Body of Christ, and is the result of two missions: that of Christ and that of the Holy Spirit. It could not be the Body of Christ without the presence of both. The anointing of Jesus as the Messiah is extended to his Body: to those who believe in him.

Read and pray over chapter 1:1-11.

Vacancy to Be Filled

The number of followers of Jesus who were together in Jerusalem was about 120. Peter took a leading role in calling for the filling of the place of Judas Iscariot. He quoted Psalm 109 as a warrant for the appointment of a successor to Judas. Jesus had fixed the number of apostles at 12, to correspond to the 12 tribes of Israel. "You will sit on thrones to judge the 12 tribes of Israel" (Lk 22:30). Judas' defection created a vacancy and the number had to be restored before the foundation of the church at Pentecost.

Read and pray over chapter 1:12-26.

When the Jewish feast of Pentecost arrived, 50 days or a week of weeks after Passover, the group of believers described in Acts 1:13-14 was gathered together in one room. This group included Mary the mother of Jesus, some other women followers of Jesus, and some of his relatives as well as the apostles. Later Judaism considered Pentecost to be the anniversary of the giving of the Law to Moses on Mount Sinai, and they deduced this from Exodus 19:1. It was a very appropriate day for the New Covenant to be finally established. At Passover the first sheaf of the barley harvest was presented to God, and fifty days later at Pentecost the first of the wheat harvest was similarly offered to the Lord. The Jews dispersed outside of Palestine came in great numbers to Jerusalem, from the distant lands inwhich they lived, to celebrate the Feast of Weeks (Pentecost). Only in the Jerusalem temple could they attend the special sacrificial ceremonial prescribed in the Book of Numbers 28:26-31.

Read and pray over chapter 2:1-13.

An Experience

There would be no developed doctrine of the Holy Spirit for a long time to come, but they experienced the Spirit as a living reality, and they saw themselves immediately as the representatives of the new reality. The Holy Spirit was a living, experienced fact for them, both as individuals and as a community. The spiritual baptism, foretold by John the Baptist and promised afresh by Jesus, was now an accomplished fact. The Spirit came and filled the disciples and Mary and the other women with his power; not like water in a bottle, but as a bubbling fresh fountain of living water which changed their lives. Whatever they saw and heard, there was no doubt about their inward experience of the Spirit.

When many great men of the Old Testament received the Spirit of Yahweh as power for their particular task, they spoke out in ecstatic praise of God. In chapter 11 of the Book of Numbers we read how Yahweh took some of the spirit which was upon Moses and gave it to the 70 elders to help Moses rule the nation. When the Spirit came upon them they began to prophesy, to speak the praises of God, to pray in tongues. Moses said on that occasion, "If only the whole people of Yahweh were prophets, and Yahweh gave his Spirit to them all" (Nm 1:29). Prophets like Ezechiel spoke in the name of

Yahweh, "I shall put my spirit in you" (Ez 36:27), and the prophet Joel spoke of the day when the Lord would pour out his Spirit on all mankind. Peter quotes this prophecy on Pentecost morning, and calls attention to its fulfillment. The crowd saw the disciples praying in tongues and mistook this ecstatic praise of God for the results of too much wine.

Read and pray over chapter 2:14-21.

You Will Be Witnesses

Jesus had told the apostles: "When the Advocate comes, whom I shall send to you from the Father, the Spirit of truth who issues from the Father, he will be my witness. And you too will be witnesses for me in Jerusalem, in all of Judea and Samaria, and to the ends of the earth" (Jn 15:20 and Acts 1:8). Peter shows that he is truly a witness and he goes on to prove from the scriptures that the Messiah must die, and rise again, and that Jesus is the Messiah. Joel had said that "all who call on the name of the Lord will be saved" (Jl 3:5), and Peter calls on his hearers to repent, turn to God, accept their sins as being forgiven, and tells them that they will receive the gift of the Holy Spirit. The Spirit of Jesus inspired his words and touched their hearts with the gift of faith in Jesus. Three thousand people joined the community that day.

Read and pray over chapter 2:22-42.

To receive the Spirit is to be in the church; to live by the power of the same Spirit means to be a member of Jesus' Risen Body. St. Paul asked a number of former disciples of John at Ephesus, "Did you receive the Spirit when you became disciples?" They didn't know there was such a thing as a Holy Spirit.

Read and pray over chapter 19:1-7.

Just as Jesus received the Spirit for the public discharge of his own messianic ministry, so now his

The Gift of the Spirit

Body receives that same anointing and his members begin to do the works he had been doing. An instance of this is the cure of the lame man in the Temple by Peter and John.

Read and pray over chapter 3:1-10.

Jesus had told John the Baptist's disciples to go back and tell him what they saw happening through his ministry, "the blind see again, the lame walk, lepers are cleansed, the deaf hear, the dead are raised to life" (Lk 7:22). These signs fulfilled the prophecies of Isaiah about the Messiah, and now that his Spirit is in his church, the same signs continue to happen through it. Peter takes the opportunity provided by the amazement of the crowd to proclaim the Good News as he had at Pentecost, but this time in the Temple. Like his Master, opposition and persecution would come to him as he followed the Spirit of Jesus and did what Jesus had done.

Read and pray over chapter 3:11 to chapter 4:4.

Points to Ponder Alone:
1. Reflect that to have received the Spirit is to be a member of the church, although not all members of the church have personally accepted him in equal measure. Some are Christians by proxy rather than from personal conviction and experience.
2. "You will be my witness." How am I to witness to the love, joy, peace, patience, kindness, goodness, trustfulness, gentleness and self-control which Jesus' Spirit brings? If I'm not much of a witness this way, where do I look for the ability to improve?

Points to Pray Privately:
1. Turn from your self-centeredness, and turn to the

Lord Jesus, so that you can accept the forgiveness he has already won for you; expect to receive the experience of the Promise of the Father. This was Peter's first message to the church.

2. The plan and purpose of God which sent Jesus and his Spirit into the world include my living a new kind of life by the Spirit of Jesus. The early church experienced a power to change, and later understood this as the presence of the Holy Spirit. I know about the Holy Spirit, but is my life much different from the life of the "world" around me?

3. The power and presence of the Holy Spirit were not just an individual experience. They knew of his action in their community life as well as in their personal life. He enabled them to love one another and be united in their faith and hope and joy.

Points to Share with the Group:

1. Share with the group what these scriptures have said to you about the Promise of the Father as the power to live like Jesus.

2. "Father, may they be one in us, as you are in me and I am in you, so that the world may believe it was you who sent me" (John 17:21). Share with the group your experiences of feeling one with this group or other groups of people. Would these experiences cause outsiders to notice that you were a different kind of people?

3. Have you ever experienced the presence of God or his power in your life? Can you share with the group how you felt, and how you knew it was the presence of God?

3
Community in the Spirit

"The eternal life which was with the Father has been made visible to us. What we have seen and heard we are telling you so that you too may be in union with us, as we are in union with the Father and with his Son Jesus Christ" (1 Jn 1:3).

Share in the Life of the Trinity

As God has revealed himself to us in the scriptures, his life and perfection are intimately bound up in the relationships and communication among the three persons of the Trinity. Where nothing else existed besides himself, he makes the universe and us begin to exist, so that he can share his life with us. He loves us into existence, and would love us into the fullness of life which Jesus came to share with us. On one of the occasions when Jesus prayed aloud to the Father in front of his disciples (shared prayer with them and with us) he said, "Everything has been entrusted to me by my Father; and no one knows the Son (in affectionate relationship) except the Father, just as no one knows the Father except the Son and those of whom the Son chooses to reveal him" (Mt 11:27). Jesus of Nazareth witnessed among us to the Father, and the person who has seen and heard Jesus has seen and heard the Father. "To have seen me is to have seen the Father ... I am in the Father and the Father is in me" (Jn 14:10). At the end of the great priestly prayer of Jesus, he prayed, "I have made your name known to them and will continue to make it known, so that the love with which you loved me (the Holy Spirit) may be in them, and so that I may be in them" (Jn 17:26). It is through the Spirit that this communion in the Father and Son is communicated outside the inner life of God, and the church is defined in relation to this communion of persons. The identification of Jesus with Christians is only possible because it is the same Holy Spirit in the Father, in the Son, and in the Christians.

Read and pray over chapter 9:1-6.

Christ "has shared with us his Spirit who, existing as one and the same being in the head and in the members, vivifies, unifies and moves the whole body" (Dogmatic Constitution on the Church, Art. 7). Thus the Body of Christ begins to do what Jesus had done. This new community way of life is described by Luke in several places.

Read and pray over chapter 4:32-37.

Unity of Purpose

The close fellowship, love for one another, and sharing of life and property, reflect something of the life of the Trinity—a life Christians share through the Spirit. As Jesus opened the eyes of the apostles to understand the scriptures concerning himself, so now the apostles were able to do the same for the new believers. Their oneness in mind and heart bore witness to something more than mere human motivation keeping them together.

Community in the Spirit

They remained faithful to the breaking of bread and met in their homes rather than in the temple for these fellowship meals. During these fellowship gatherings they praised God, shared whatever they had, and did in commemoration of Jesus what he had done at the Last Supper. The word Eucharist means thanksgiving and describes very well this communal sharing and praise. The fellowship was the oneness Jesus had prayed about after the Last Supper. "With me in them and you in me, may they be so completely one that the world will realize that it was you who sent me and that I have loved them as much as you loved me" (Jn 17:23). Their unity of purpose not only prompted them to share all their material goods on a voluntary basis, but it also made any deception or pretense unthinkable. When Ananias and Sapphira sold some property and made a big show of giving *all* of the proceeds to the community, while they were actually only giving a part of the money, a startling sign was given to the community.

Read and pray over chapter 5:1-11.

Unity, Love and Trust

Signs like this made the community take the Lord's word seriously and a reverential fear turned them more earnestly to him. Many other signs and miracles came from the ministry of the apostles. The people rushed to bring their sick relatives and friends to the apostles, because all the sick and possessed who came were cured. Even the shadow of Peter falling on sick people in the streets caused the healing power of Jesus to enter their bodies and minds.

Read and pray over chapter 5:12-16.

Just as jealously, fear and self-interest had brought persecution to Jesus during his ministry, so now the same thing happened to his disciples. First of all, it was because they were preaching the resurrection of Jesus from the dead. They were arrested, held overnight, and brought before the Great Sanhedrin of Jerusalem to be interrogated. The Holy Spirit moved Peter, an uneducated layman, to preach the Good News even to Israel's supreme court.

Read and pray over chapter 4:1-17.

Jesus had promised the apostles: "But when they hand you over, do not worry about how to speak or what to say; what you are to say will be given to you when the time comes; because it is not you who will be speaking; the Spirit of your Father will be speaking in you" (Mt 10:19-20). The assurance shown by Peter and John astonished the Jewish leaders, and they couldn't escape the fact that a cured man was standing by the side of the apostles. They gave them a solemn legal warning, since they were first offenders.

Read and pray over chapter 4:18-22.

Peter and John had retorted that they must listen to God rather than to men in this matter, and that they could not promise to refrain from proclaiming the Good News as they had been ordered. The warnings were repeated and they were released. As soon as they were free, they went to the community, which joined them in prayer. Their prayers were answered immediately as the Spirit manifested his presence again.

Read and pray over chapter 4:23-31.

As they continued to preach in the power of the Spirit, they were very soon arrested again, and put in the common jail. However, the Lord opened the prison gates and told them to go and stand in the Temple and continue preaching. When their captors sent for them next morning and found the prison securely locked but empty, they wondered what it could mean.

Read and pray over chapter 5:17-26.

Peter and the other apostles used their second appearance before the Sanhedrin to witness again to

Community in the Spirit

Jesus as Lord and Savior. As usual, the only answer to the Truth, when men do not want to accept it, is violence. However, Gamaliel the Elder intervened with sound wisdom. He was a much respected pharisaic leader and the greatest teacher of his day. Saul of Tarsus was one of his disciples. He suggested a wait-and-see policy, and warned against acting contrary to something which might be of God.

Read and pray over chapter 5:27-42.

Despite the repeated warning and a flogging, the apostles continued to preach in the Temple and in private homes. Their proclamation of the Good News of Christ Jesus was never interrupted. The community's obedience to God certainly came before its obedience to men, and through its faith the power of the Spirit was released into the world.

Read and pray over chapter 9:10-31.

When King Herod started persecuting the church in Jerusalem and beheaded James, Peter was next on the list. He was arrested, imprisoned, and heavily guarded. When the angel of the Lord led him to freedom, he turned to the community which had been praying for him, and then he went into hiding.

Read and pray over chapter 12:1-19.

Points to Ponder Alone:

1. After telling us that we must love our enemies and pray for those who persecute us, Jesus said, "You must therefore be perfect just as your heavenly Father is perfect" (Mt 5:48). The only way I can be perfect like the Father is to accept a share in his life. I can only be godlike through the gift of his godliness.

2. So many trivial things can separate us from other people, and yet Jesus prayed that his disciples be able to be one as he and the Father and the Spirit are One. In the power of the Spirit, this oneness was very evident in the apostolic church.

Points to Pray Privately:

1. Ask Jesus for the power of his Spirit to be able to love, to share and to be happy with other people as were the early members of the church.

2. Worshiping together, especially in the Breaking of Bread, was the way they expressed their faith in the Father's love for them. Thanksgiving (Eucharistia) and praise of God for his promises and faithfulness to them brought abundant experience of God's goodness.

3. "No one knows the Son except the Father . . . no one knows the Father except the Son, and those to whom the Son chooses to reveal him." This is the affectionate relationship which is so much a part of the life of the Trinity as revealed to us. Then Jesus says to the Father, "I have loved them as much as you have loved me." Finally, he says, "Love one another, as I have loved you."

Points to Share with the Group:

1. Share what your readings have said to you about your sharing in the life of God.

2. The apostles were full of joy at suffering disgrace for the name of Jesus. What kind of joy do you think this was, and do you think it is possible to accept persecution and discrimination in the joy of Jesus' love?

3. Do you feel the need for Christian community support? Share with your group how you feel about this, and what you think can be done about it.

4
Mission

"The disciples were filled with joy when they saw the Lord, and he said to them again; 'Peace be with you. As the Father sent me, so am I sending you' " (Jn 20:21).

So Am I Sending You

Scripture tells us that the Father sent the Son, and that Jesus willingly submitted to being sent by God as the sacrificial Lamb who redeems mankind. In the Trinity there is unity and equality and perfect ability to relate without conflict. However, the Father exercises headship in expressing the common purpose of all three Persons, and the Son submits to being sent, as does the Holy Spirit. The Son and the Spirit express this common purpose of the Trinity by submission, and reveal to us the way for us to share in the life of God. In the Spirit of Jesus the apostles understood the mystery of God's purpose of love, and accepted being sent by Jesus so that this might come about. In their turn, they would send others who had embraced this saving plan, and who had been enabled by the Spirit to surrender their lives to Jesus, as Jesus did to the Father.

Read and pray over chapter 6:1-7.

The church of Jerusalem comprised both Hebrews (Aramaic-speaking Jews, most of whom were natives of Palestine) and Hellenists (Jews whose habitual language was Greek, many of whom were natives of Greco-Roman lands). There was a tension between these two groups and this expressed itself in the trifling matter of the distribution of alms to the poor. Widows formed a considerable proportion of the poor in the church community, and the Hellenist widows complained of discrimination, because the Hebrews controlled the distribution. The apostles called a community meeting to set things right. They asked the community to select seven men capable of doing the job. The seven men selected all have Greek names which suggests that they belonged to the Hellenistic group. One of them, Nicolaus of Antioch, was a Proselyte or convert from paganism. The whole community selected them and then the apostles "missioned" them by praying over them and laying hands on them. These seven almoners were not restricted to just handing out food; Stephen and Philip worked as well in evangelism and for the defense of the faith.

Read and pray over chapter 6:8-15.

The Spirit of Wisdom in Stephen

Stephen worked so powerfully that the only answer to his ministry was violence, and he was the first of the followers of Jesus to "drink the cup" that Jesus had to drink. His speech is the prototype of Christian apologetic against the Jews. It is designed to demonstrate to them that Christianity and not Judaism is the true fulfillment of the revelation given through Moses and the prophets. If you don't have much background in the Old Testament you could omit reading this speech without missing much of the main story. However, why not try reading slowly and prayerfully.

Read and pray over chapter 7:1-53.

Everywhere else in the New Testament the Messiah is seen as seated at the right hand of the Father, but Stephen sees him standing. Stephen had been confessing Christ before men as a witness, and now he sees Christ confessing his servant before God. The proper posture for a witness was the standing posture. Stephen's reference to Jesus as "Son of Man" is the only place in the New Testament when anyone but Jesus uses this term. Stephen grasped and asserted that Jesus is the way of access to God in a more immediate and personally satisfying way than the obsolete temple ritual had ever been able to provide. The age of particular favor for the Jewish nation was over, and the Messiah's sovereignty embraces all nations without distinction.

Read and pray over chapters 7:54 to 8:3.

From the time of the settlement of the promised land, the isolation of the tribe of Judah from the northern tribes of Israel led to long-standing differences between the populations of Judea and Samaria. After the exile these differences widened, when the Samaritans erected a temple on Gerizim to rival the restored Temple at Jerusalem. Judeans regarded the Samaritans as racial and religious half-breeds. They had assimilated foreign settlers planted in Samaria by the Assyrians after the fall of the northern kingdom. Jesus had told the disciples they would be his witnesses not only in Jerusalem but throughout Judea and Samaria (Acts 1:8). Now Philip, one of the seven almoners missioned with Stephen, is driven from his work in Jerusalem and goes north to preach the gospel in Samaria.

Read and pray over chapter 8:4-13.

The apostles had remained behind in Jerusalem, despite the persecution, and when they heard that the Samaritans had accepted the Good News, they sent

Peter and John to Samaria. They prayed for the Samaritans to receive the Holy Spirit and laid hands on them. The imposition of hands was not necessarily sacramental confirmation, but primarily a token of fellowship and solidarity. The results were so spectacular that Simon the Magician offered to buy the "trick" from Peter. He received a sharp rebuke for his effort, and is remembered in church vocabulary by the term "simony" which refers to the unworthy buying and selling of ecclesiastical offices.

Read and pray over chapter 8:14-25.

After the incident with Simon the Magician, Philip went back to Jerusalem with Peter and John, evangelizing other Samaritan communities as they went. In Jerusalem the Spirit of the Lord (also called here the angel of the Lord) spoke to Philip, and gave him directions to meet an Ethiopian. The man was probably a God-fearing Gentile who had visited Jerusalem as a worshiper. He was a eunuch employed as a court official in Ethiopia.

Read and pray over chapter 8:26-40.

Sent to Preach

Later we shall see Peter missioned or sent by the Holy Spirit to Cornelius and the pagans (chapters 10 and 11). Also Barnabas was sent by the church at Jerusalem to Antioch. Barnabas went to Tarsus to look for Saul and brought him back to Antioch to help him found the church there. The Church of Antioch sent Barnabas and Saul to Judea with money for the poor, and later this church would send them to preach the Good News in Asia Minor (chapter 13:2-3).

Read and pray over chapter 11:19-30.

The mission of the church is in great part defined in terms of the world in which it is present. The disciples are sent to preach to Jews (both Hebrews and

Hellenists), to Samaritans, to God-fearers, to Proselytes (Gentiles who believed and worshipped in the Old Testament faith) and to pagans. This mission was in the church's witness by life, love, and worship to the abiding and saving presence of God among men. It was the living community of reconciliation which made known the Good News, and this is what the Spirit enabled the church to be.

Read and pray over chapter 2:43-47.

"Go out to the whole world; proclaim the Good News to all creation. He who believes and is baptized will be saved; he who does not believe will be condemned. These are the signs that will be associated with believers: in my name they will cast out devils; they will have the gift of tongues; they will pick up snakes in their hands, and be unharmed should they drink deadly poison; they will lay their hands on the sick, who will recover" (Mk 16:16-18).

Points to Ponder Alone:
1. Think of authority as the proclamation of the common purpose of the family or community by the person in headship. Think of obedience as subscribing to that common purpose by being submissive to it, as Jesus was submissive to the Father.
2. Jesus sent his disciples to do simple everyday things, besides the big things like preaching and miracles. He sent them to love, to serve, to share, to be happy, to bring peace, etc. Think about your mission from Jesus and the things he sends you to do.

Points to Pray Privately:
1. "If our life in Christ means anything to you, if love can persuade at all, or the Spirit that we have in

common, or any tenderness or sympathy, then be united in your convictions and united in your love, with a common purpose and a common mind. There must be no competition among you, no conceit; but everybody is to be self-effacing. In your minds you must be the same as Christ Jesus" (Phil 2:1-5).
2. How much rebellion is there in my life to the truth, beauty, and glory of God expressed in the lives of others? Do I praise him for his goodness, or do I react like Stephen's hearers with anger, jealousy, denigration, negative humor, obstruction . . . ?
3. There were many people who were discriminated against for no reason except that they belonged to different religious or ethnic groups (Hebrews, Hellenists, Samaritans, pagans, Gentiles). Are there classes or categories of people to whom I do not give justice in thought or act because I "don't like them"?

Points to Share with the Group:
1. Share how you feel about accepting your mission in life? What do you see Jesus sending you to do, or to be? How do you accept your present situation as part of that mission?
2. Share what the scriptures have said to you about authority, obedience, surrender, submission, and fidelity in the Christian community or family.
3. How you feel about obstruction, rugged individualism, discrimination, persecution, and anti-government attitudes in the kingdom of God?

5
Salvation for Pagans

Proselytes and God-fearers

There were two classes of Gentile followers of the Jewish faith, the Proselytes and the God-fearers. Proselytes were Gentile converts who accepted Judaism in its entirety. Gentiles who did this were initiated into a new way of life which implied a change of citizenship by circumcision, ritual bath or baptism, and the offering of a sacrificial victim. Nicolaus of Antioch, one of the seven helpers missioned by the apostles (chapter 6), was a convert of Judaism, a Proselyte. God-fearers were Gentiles who accepted Jewish teaching but did not accept circumcision and change of citizenship. The Ethiopian who was baptized by Philip on the road to Gaza was a God-fearer, and so were Cornelius and his family at Caesarea who were baptized by Peter. They were ruled by a set of laws known as the Precept of Noah, embodying the few things required of a Gentile to be able to associate with Jews, so that the Jews would not incur ceremonial ineligibilities.

The Good News of Salvation had been preached to Jews and Proselytes at Pentecost by the apostles (Acts 2:11) as well as to a few individual God-fearers. These people could almost be considered part of the Jewish nation. The Samaritans were considered heretics, but they were still not completely outside the fold. Now we are going to follow the extension of the kingdom to the pagans.

Truth Revealed to Peter

Following in the footsteps of his Master, Peter travelled to Lydda, a city on the seacoast of Palestine, where he preached the Gospel and healed the sick. At Joppa, a coastal town nearby, he visited the Christian community and raised Tabitha from the dead. From there he was called by the Spirit to Caesarea to learn the truth about salvation for the pagans.

Read and pray over chapter 9:31-43.

A centurion in the Roman army was nominally in charge of 100 men, and although his status was that of a noncommissioned officer, he was the equivalent of a modern army captain. The centurions who appear in the New Testament are all fine men, and the first Gentile with whom Jesus had dealings in his public ministry was a Roman centurion who asked him to cure his servant (Mt 8:11). The first Gentile that Peter has to deal with in his public ministry is also a centurion. In the mainly Gentile city of Caesarea, there lived a centurion of one of the auxiliary cohorts in Judea named Cornelius, who was a God-fearer.

Read and pray over chapter 10:1-8.

Peter Has a Vision

Guidance concerning Jewish food laws is given to Peter in a vision, but he soon grasped that it had much wider applications. Jesus had said, "Nothing that goes into a man from outside can make him unclean; it is the things that come out of a man (evil intentions of his heart) that make him unclean" (Mk 7:14-23). Peter must have heard that, but now he begins to understand it. This was an abrogation of ceremonial food laws and many similar barriers.

Read and pray over chapter 10:9-23

A God-fearer had no objection to the company of Jews, but no orthodox Jew would willingly enter a Gentile dwelling. Peter invited the messengers from Cornelius into Simon the Tanner's house to share his meal, and he provided accommodation for them overnight. The next day he and some of the men of the Joppa community went back with the messengers to Caesarea.

Pentecost of the Gentiles

On arrival, Peter and Cornelius shared their experiences, and Peter realized that it was the hand of the Lord bringing them together. He began to proclaim the Gospel to them, and as he spoke, the Pentecost of the Gentile world took place.

Read and pray over chapter 10:24-48.

Their obvious reception of the Spirit indicated their membership in the Body of Christ, and so Peter ordered them to be baptized and welcomed into the Christian community.

Peter Justifies His Action

When rumors of what Peter had done reached the church in Jerusalem, the elders were upset at this departure from traditional Jewish practice. On his return home Peter had to explain what had happened, and his account satisfied them.

Read and pray over chapter 11:1-18.

The Church at Antioch

Luke's story now jumps back to the persecution which followed Stephen's martyrdom (Acts 8:4). Some of the scattered believers ended up hundreds of miles north in Syria, at Antioch. It was the third-largest city in the known world at this time, and had a large Jewish community. There they preached not only to the Jews, but also directly to the Gentiles. The church in Jerusalem heard about this, and sent Barnabas to investigate. He saw the obvious hand of God in what was happening, and called in Saul of Tarsus to help him establish the church there.

Read and pray over chapter 11:19-30.

Association with Gentiles

Some years later, when Paul and Barnabas returned to Syrian Antioch after the first great missionary journey to Asia Minor, a dispute broke out in that church. Some men from Judea came to Antioch and insisted that the Gentile members of the church be circumcised and accept the traditions of Moses. Did Christians all have to observe the Law of the Old Testament? Paul and Barnabas argued that they did not, but things grew into such a confrontation that delegations were sent to the church in Jerusalem to discuss the problem with the elders there. The result was the Council of Jerusalem, the first council of the church.

Read and pray over chapter 15:1-21.

The Spirit was certainly present, and what looked like being a hot debate was guided by Peter and James into a consensus that Gentiles be not bound to obey the Old Law. However, there was a problem in a "mixed" church where Jewish Christians, who wished to observe the Law, had to associate with Gentile Christians who did not observe it. Out of sensitivity and love for their Jewish brothers, the Gentile Christians were asked to abstain from things which would make it difficult for observing Jews to be in community with them and still be eligible for Jewish ceremonial worship. The apostles decided to send delegates to Antioch with a letter explaining the decision to the church there. Judas and Silas were leading members of the Jerusalem church and their verbal testimony would add weight to the letter. The opponents of Paul and Barnabas could not doubt that they were getting the truth from Jerusalem.

Read and pray over chapter 15:22-35.

Points to Ponder Alone:

1. a) "Before the world was made, he chose us in Christ, to be holy and spotless, and to live through love in his presence,
   b) determining that we should become his adopted sons through Jesus Christ,
   c) in whom, through his blood, we gain our freedom, the forgiveness of our sins.
   d) He has let us know the mystery of his purpose, that he would bring everything together under Christ as head" (Eph 1:4-10).

   These four blessings come to us in Christ, and are intended for all men and women regardless of color, race or social status.

2. The Holy Spirit, who guided Peter and Cornelius to the truth, is ever present in the Body of Christ as a whole, and in each member in his or her individuality. He continues to guide by his inspirations; sometimes in visions or feeling experiences, sometimes by circumstances.

Points to Pray Privately:

1. "We know that by turning everything to their good God cooperates with all those who love him" (Rom 8:28). How readily do I see the hand of God in things

that happen to me, and how often do I thank him for his providence when I recognize it?
2. Have you ever been asked to give up doing something for no other reason than it makes life more pleasant for someone else? The apostolic church of Jews and Gentiles accepted such demands in love. Do I have the love and "readiness to serve" that would help other people to see the community to which I belong as a fraternity of love?
3. How much do jealousy and self-preservation keep me from "washing other people's feet"? Can I really be glad at their success and rejoice in their happiness?

Points to Share with the Group:
1. Share with your group what these scriptures have said to you.
2. Can you be universal in your desire for happiness for everyone, just the way God is? "He causes his sun to rise on bad men as well as good!" Share with the group what you feel about loving everyone, even those who harm you.
3. Is the Christian community you belong to an outgoing expression of God's love and concern for everyone, or is it a fear-ridden survival-seeking collection of selfish people?

6
Paul

"This man is my chosen instrument to bring my name before pagans and pagan kings and before the people of Israel" (Acts 9:15).

Persecution

The death of Stephen was the beginning of a campaign of repression against the Jerusalem church. The Hellenists in the community seem to have been the main target and were forced to leave Jerusalem; the church there became predominantly Hebrew from that time on. A principal figure in the repressive campaign was Saul of Tarsus, who had authority from the Sanhedrin to track down and arrest members of the new movement.

Read and pray over chapters 8:1-4 and 9:1-2.

Vocation of Paul

While he was on his way to Damascus, zealously defending the ways of God, Saul was given a revelation that was to transform his whole life. It was more of a call to new service in the Lord than a conversion from a sinful way of life. There are three accounts of his vision in Acts, one narrated by Luke and two spoken by Paul in his speeches; this threefold repetition highlights the importance of the event. As in the case of Peter and Cornelius (chapter 10), both Ananias and Saul are directed by a vision to bring about the inauguration of Saul as a prophet of the Good News to the nations.

"I, Yahweh, have called you to serve the cause of right; I have taken you by the hand and formed you; I have appointed you as covenant of the people and light of the nations, to open the eyes of the blind, to free captives from prison, and those who live in darkness from the dungeon" (Is 42:6-7).

Ananias and the community of believers at Damascus showed the fruits of the presence of Jesus' Spirit among them, as they welcomed and cared for the "archenemy" who had been persecuting them.

Read and pray over chapters 9:3-25, 22:1-21 and 26:9-18.

Barnabas

When Saul went to Jerusalem to visit the apostles, they were naturally very suspicious of him. It was Barnabas, a generous Levite of Cypriot origin, described in chapter 4:36-37, who took Saul under his wing and introduced him to the apostles. When Saul started preaching in Jerusalem, the Hellenistic Jews determined to kill him; so the Christian community got him out of the way, and sent him to Tarsus. Later, when the Jerusalem church sent Barnabas to Antioch to supervise the establishment of the community there, Barnabas went to Tarsus to find Saul. When he found him, he took him back to Antioch where they lived together for over a year instructing the Christian community. It was here that the disciples of Jesus were first called

"Christians." They lived by the same spirit as Christ, the anointed One.

Read and pray over chapters 9:26-30 and 11:19-30.

The Church at Antioch

After their journey to Jerusalem with money from the church at Antioch, Barnabas and Saul returned to Antioch, where they were listed as two of the acknowledged prophets and teachers governing the local community. During their community prayer one day, there was an inspired utterance in which the Holy Spirit prompted someone to prophesy that Barnabas and Saul were to be set aside for a special mission. The community discerned this message by praying about it and keeping a fast and they concluded by laying hands on Barnabas and Saul and sending them forth to follow the promptings of the Spirit. First of all, they headed for Barnabas' homeland of Cyprus.

Read and pray over chapters 12:24 to 13:12.

Mission to Asia Minor (Turn to Map 1, page 57)

Having evangelized part of Barnabas' native island, they decided to cross to the south coast of Paul's native land, Asia Minor. Up to this point Barnabas had always been mentioned first in the account Luke gives, and naturally an original member of the Jerusalem church like Barnabas would be thought of as the leader of the mission. However, from the time they set foot on the mainland (modern Turkey), Paul seems to take over the leadership and is always mentioned first. "Barnabas and Saul" changes to "Paul and his company." They eventually arrived at Antioch in Pisidia (not to be confused with their home community of Antioch in Syria). It was a Roman colony with a well-established Jewish community. On the first sabbath of their stay there, they headed for the synagogue and joined the congregation in worship.

Read and pray over chapter 13:13-43.

To the Pagans

When the synagogue officials invited them to speak, Paul didn't need a second invitation, and proceeded to move directly from David to Christ in his speech. The result was quite favorable, and he was asked to speak again on the same theme. Everybody in town came on the next Sabbath to hear Paul speak. However, the local Jewish leaders became jealous and contradicted everything he said. Eventually, Paul and Barnabas shook the dust from their feet and headed for Iconium. Their opponents would continue to obstruct their mission in the other towns they evangelized, by following them and preaching against them.

Read and pray over chapter 13:44-52.

Persecution

At Iconium they began again in the synagogue, but eventually had to move on to Lystra and Derbe. Despite the miracle worked at Lystra by curing the cripple, the Jews from Antioch and Iconium managed to turn the crowd against Paul, and he nearly lost his life there.

Read and pray over chapter 14:1-20.

Return to Antioch in Syria

Paul must have been very hardy because, despite being almost stoned to death, he set out next day for Derbe. He decided to return to Antioch in Syria by retracing his steps, rather than by going straight back through Tarsus. This made it possible for him to encourage and instruct all the new Christians in Iconium and Pisidian Antioch. The missionary tour had occupied the best part of a year and they gave an enthusiastic account to the community when they arrived home.

Read and pray over chapter 14:21-28.

Points to Ponder Alone:

1. To be a Christian means to share the anointing of Christ; the power and presence of the Holy Spirit which came upon him after his baptism in the Jordan.
2. "Talk to other people, to their improvement, their encouragement, and their consolation" (1 Cor 14:3). This is how Paul describes the role of prophecy in the community, and it is what he lives out in his prophetic mission. He chooses to go back into danger to encourage new Christians, rather than take a safe way home via Tarsus.

Points to Pray Privately:

1. The Holy Spirit must have been a powerful reality in the lives of people like Ananias and Saul.
2. Barnabas acted as a kind of godparent or sponsor for Saul in Jerusalem, and opened the way into the life of the apostolic community at Jerusalem for him. He accepted the leadership of the very person he had brought into the community. Think about how a veteran Christian and foundation member like Barnabas could make way for the chosen instrument of God, Saul of Tarsus.
3. Reflect on the church at Antioch prayerfully listening to the prophetic word, judging its authenticity by prayer and fasting, and acting on the instruction to send forth Barnabas and Saul.

Points to Share with the Group:

1. Share anything the scriptures you read may have said to you about responding to the call of God in your life.
2. What does the sense of community at Antioch say to you about obedience to the will of God, con-

sciousness of belonging to the Body of Christ, and accountability to those in headship?
3. What is the source of the zeal and missionary thrust of the new Christian communities described in Acts?

7
To Europe

"And so, while the Jews demand miracles, and the Greeks look for wisdom, here are we preaching a crucified Christ; to the Jews an obstacle they cannot get over, to the pagans madness, but to those who have been called, whether they are Jews or Greeks, a Christ who is the power and the wisdom of God" (1 Cor 1:22-24).

The Disagreement (Turn to Map 2, page 59)

After the Council of Jerusalem, Paul and Barnabas spent some time back in Antioch, and then they decided to return and visit again the communities they had evangelized in Asia Minor. However, a quarrel erupted between Paul and Barnabas over taking John Mark with them. Paul probably thought that John Mark had deserted them at Perga during their first journey (Acts 13:13) and refused to take him along. Barnabas, who was John Mark's cousin, insisted on taking him with them. So they separated, with Paul going back to his native Cilicia, and Barnabas and John Mark heading for Cyprus. Paul chose as his companion Silas, one of the deputation from the Jerusalem church who had come to Antioch with the Council document. It would be an advantage for Paul to have a member of the Jerusalem church as his companion, one who was also a Roman citizen like himself. The story of this argument between Paul and Barnabas is honestly narrated by Luke and he makes no judgment as to who was in the wrong. Even the apostolic church, in the full power of the Spirit, is still human and imperfect.

Timothy, True Child of Mine in Faith

Paul travelled overland from Antioch to Tarsus, and then on through Derbe to Lystra. There he decided to take a second travelling companion with him, a young man named Timothy. Timothy and his mother, Eunice, had been converted to Christianity during Paul's first visit, and he was destined to become one of Paul's most intimate and trusted associates. As far as the Jews were concerned, Timothy was a Gentile because he was the uncircumcised son of a Greek. However, the Gentiles saw him as a Jew because he had been brought up in his mother's religion. Paul regularized his standing in Jewish circles by circumcising him. This particular instance did not compromise the stand Paul took about Gentile Christians not being obliged to submit to circumcision and other aspects of the Old Law.

Read and pray over chapters 15:35 to 16:5.

The Vision—Call to Europe

There is a keen sensitivity to the guidance of the Spirit of God in Paul's missionary journeys, and the vision of a Macedonian leads him to take the Gospel into Europe. It is interesting that at this point (Acts 16:10) the author must have joined the party as a fourth member, because the story continues in the first person instead of the third person. This is the first of the "we" sections of the book. They travelled by sea and came to Philippi in Macedonia.

Read and pray over chapter 16:6-15.

Deliverance

When Paul delivered the slave girl from possession by an evil spirit, he ruined a profitable business for her owners. The irate businessmen called in the arm of the law and Paul and Silas were flogged and thrown in prison without a trial or hearing. The Lord in his turn delivered them from evil, and brought light and life to the jailer and his family.

Read and pray over chapter 17:1-33.

Persecution by the Jews

At Philippi, as on several other occasions, Roman citizenship proved useful to Paul and Silas. However, they had to move on to avoid further trouble, and they left Lydia's hospitality for Thessalonica. It was the same story of Jewish jealousy organizing persecution as soon as the word began to take root. They had to move on again, this time to Berea. The people there were more open to the Gospel, but it was not long before mob violence was stirred up against them. Paul ended up in Athens where he took the opportunity to preach to the Greek philosophers.

Read and pray over chapter 17:1-33.

To the Gentiles

After his time at Athens, Paul went on to Corinth, where he met Aquila and Priscilla and lodged with them. Silas and Timothy joined him, and the usual plan of preaching to the Jews in their synagogues was followed. The usual opposition and persecution came, so Paul announced that from that time on he would go to the Gentiles directly. He set up his teaching center in a Gentile house and carried on the mission. He spent about a year and a half in Corinth, and after a brief and successful visit to Ephesus, he sailed for Jerusalem and his "base community" in Syria at Antioch. Thus ended his second missionary journey.

Read and pray over chapter 18:1-23.

Paul's Third Journey (Turn to Map 3, page 61)

Paul had promised the Ephesians that he would come back to them. He set out overland again, and preached his way through the Christian communities of Asia Minor until he was back at Ephesus. The Holy Spirit was sent to teach them everything and to remind them of all that Jesus had said. Apollos and the disciples of John were led to the whole truth through Priscilla, Aquila and Paul. The power of the Spirit worked so strongly through Paul that even his clothing was the channel of healing and deliverance.

Read and pray over chapters 18:24 to 19:20.

Whenever the power of the Gospel affected the pockets of the pagans Paul found himself in real trouble. The owners of the fortune-telling slave girl at Philippi had him run out of town, and now the silversmiths of Ephesus find him reducing the market for statues and idols. Paul had to leave town again.

Read and pray over chapter 19:21-41.

After a few months in Greece, confirming the faith of the churches there, he came back to Ephesus through Troas. He gave a great farewell exhortation to the Ephesian elders and set out for Jerusalem.

Read and pray over chapter 20:1-38.

Points to Ponder Alone:
1. "And so, while the Jews demanded miracles and the Greeks look for wisdom, here are we preaching a crucified Christ; to the Jews an obstacle that they

cannot get over, to the pagans madness, but to those who have been called, whether they are Jews or Greeks, a Christ who is the power and wisdom of God" (1 Cor 1:22-24).

2. In what way could the Spirit of Jesus work through me? In what ways could I be a channel of new life and freedom to others?

Points to Pray Privately:

1. That the Lord might free me from the blindness of pride, ambition, jealousy, and the rest of my sinfulness, so that I can hear his voice.
2. That I might recognize my hostilities to other people before they become a source of disagreement and quarrels, and that I claim the power of Jesus' Spirit to be loving as he is loving.
3. That hardship, suffering, and persecution might not prevent me being an expression of love and concern for others.

Points to Share with the Group:

1. What do you see as the main causes of disagreement and quarrels among Christians in their relationships with one another?
2. What did the scriptures you read say to you about yourself and the church?
3. What have you noticed about the zeal of the early Christian communities and their missionaries? How are present-day Christians different from early Christians?

8
To Rome in Chains

"Yahweh had been pleased to crush him with suffering. If he offers his life in atonement, he shall see his heirs, he shall have a long life and through him what Yahweh wishes will be done" (Is 53:10).

Suffering Servants

The prophets foretold the sufferings of the Messiah long before he came on earth, and Jesus knew of these prophecies. After he had elicited from his disciples the first explicit profession of faith in him as Messiah, he went on "to make it clear to them that he was destined to go to Jerusalem and suffer grievously at the hands of the elders and chief priests and scribes, and to be put to death" (Mt 16:21). The Holy Spirit made it clear to Paul that he too would have to suffer.

Read and pray over chapters 20:22-24 and 21:1-16.

Just as the Son of God had expressed his complete involvement in the plan of the Trinity by being sent to play his part as the Christ, so Paul was able to do the same thing in the Spirit of Jesus. Jesus had prayed:

"Father, if you are willing, take this cup away from me. Nevertheless, let your will be done, not mine" (Lk 22:42). Paul spoke to the Philippians about this when he said: "In your minds you must be the same as Christ Jesus: His state was divine, yet he did not cling to his equality with God but emptied himself to assume the condition of a slave, and became as men are; he was humbler yet, even to accepting death on a cross. But God raised him high and gave him the name which is above all other names, so that all beings in the heavens, on earth and in the underworld, should bend the knee at the name of Jesus, and that every tongue should acclaim Jesus Christ as Lord, to the glory of God the Father" (Phil 2:5-11).

Visit to Jerusalem

Paul received a warm welcome from the elders of the Jerusalem church, and they praised God for what he had done through Paul. However, they were worried for Paul's safety, because false rumors relating to the abolition of Jewish customs supposedly taught by Paul had inflamed some of the conservative Jewish Christions. They suggested that Paul let himself be seen in the Temple, worshipping as a pious and observant Jew fulfilling ancestral customs. It was proposed that he join four of their number, who had contracted some ceremonial defilement and undertaken a temporary Nazarite vow. He would seek purification with them and pay the expenses of their sacrifice offerings.

Read and pray over chapter 21:17-40.

Arrested in the Temple

Even under Roman rule there was still a death penalty for any Gentile who dared enter the "Court of Israel," and his enemies mistakenly assumed that Paul had brought Trophimus into the restricted area. Paul could be grateful for the Roman concern for peace and good order, as the troops probably saved his life. When Paul was given permission to address the crowd he spoke in Hebrew, and this quieted the mob for a while, but the Romans soon had to get him out of the way.

Read and pray over chapter 22:1-30.

Prisoner in Chains

Jesus told Peter that "when you were young you put on your own belt and walked where you liked; but when you grow old you will stretch out your hands, and someone else will put a belt round you and take you where you would rather not go" (Jn 21:18). Paul began this experience at Jerusalem and it would last for several years and end up in Rome. It must have been a great suffering for a zealous, itinerant evangelist like Paul to spend all that time in "useless" captivity. However, he had previously written to the Romans during his third journey:

"How rich are the depths of God—how deep his wisdom and knowledge—and how impossible to penetrate his motives or understand his methods. Who could ever know the mind of the Lord? Who could ever be his counsellor? Who could ever give him anything or lend him anything? All that exists comes from him; all is by him and for him.To him be glory for ever" (Rom 11:33-36).

Now he would give witness by putting into practice what he had preached, and he was comforted by the Lord in a vision.

Read and pray over chapter 23:1-35.

Appeal to Caesar

Paul pleaded his case before Felix, but he was kept in custody for two years at Caesarea. He should have been released from preventive custody then, but a change of governors came at the same time. When it looked as though the new governor, Festus, might hand him over to the Jews to gain their favor, Paul exercised his right as a Roman citizen and appealed to Caesar, to the supreme court. Festus used him to entertain King Agrippa, and Paul used the occasion to preach the Truth.

Read and pray over chapters 25:1-27 and 26:24-32.

Shipwreck on Malta (Turn to Map 4, page 63)

Luke must have traveled to Rome with Paul, as the "we" section, which began at chapter 20, continues here as a firsthand account of the journey. Although a prisoner in chains, Paul is presented as the leading figure in the major events of the journey, and the Spirit of Jesus gives him prophetic knowledge of things to come. With the aid of the map you can trace the voyage from Caesarea to Malta.

Read and pray over chapters 27:1 to 28:10.

Rome at Last

Paul had written to the Romans: "For I want very much to see you in order to share a spiritual blessing with you to make you strong. What I mean is that both you and I will be helped at the same time, you by my faith and I by your faith" (Rom 1:11-12). He was to spend two years among them doing just that. He had come to the center of the world of that time, where he would continue to proclaim the Gospel to all who visited him.

Read and pray over chapter 28:11-31.

Points to Ponder Alone:

1. To accept the kingdom of God means to accept my part in its coming about. "Who can know the mind of the Lord, so who can teach him? But we are those who have the mind of Christ" (1 Cor 2:16).

2. The Way taught by Jesus included persecution, suffering and death for each one of his followers. Because of what he has done I can face them with confidence and joy, but I must accept them as he accepted his Father's will.

Points to Pray Privately:

1. Ask for the light and strength to be able to say with Jesus: "Here I am! I am coming to obey your will" (Heb 10:9).
2. Pray that you can accept the mystery of God's plan and purpose in your life, especially when you can't see any reason for your pain and suffering.
3. "You did not see him (in your trial and suffering), yet you love him; and still without seeing him, you are already filled with a joy so glorious that it cannot be described, because you believe; and you are sure of the end to which your faith looks forward, that is, the salvation of your souls" (1 Pt 1:8-9).

Points to Share with the Group:

1. Share with your group what the story of Paul's fourth journey said to you about his personal involvement in the plan of God.
2. Share what the scriptures said to you about acceptance of pain and suffering in apostolic Christian life.
3. "How impossible to penetrate his motives or to understand his methods" (Rom 11:33). Share with your group what the mystery of the changeless love of God means to you in the face of pain and evil and suffering in the world.

Map 1

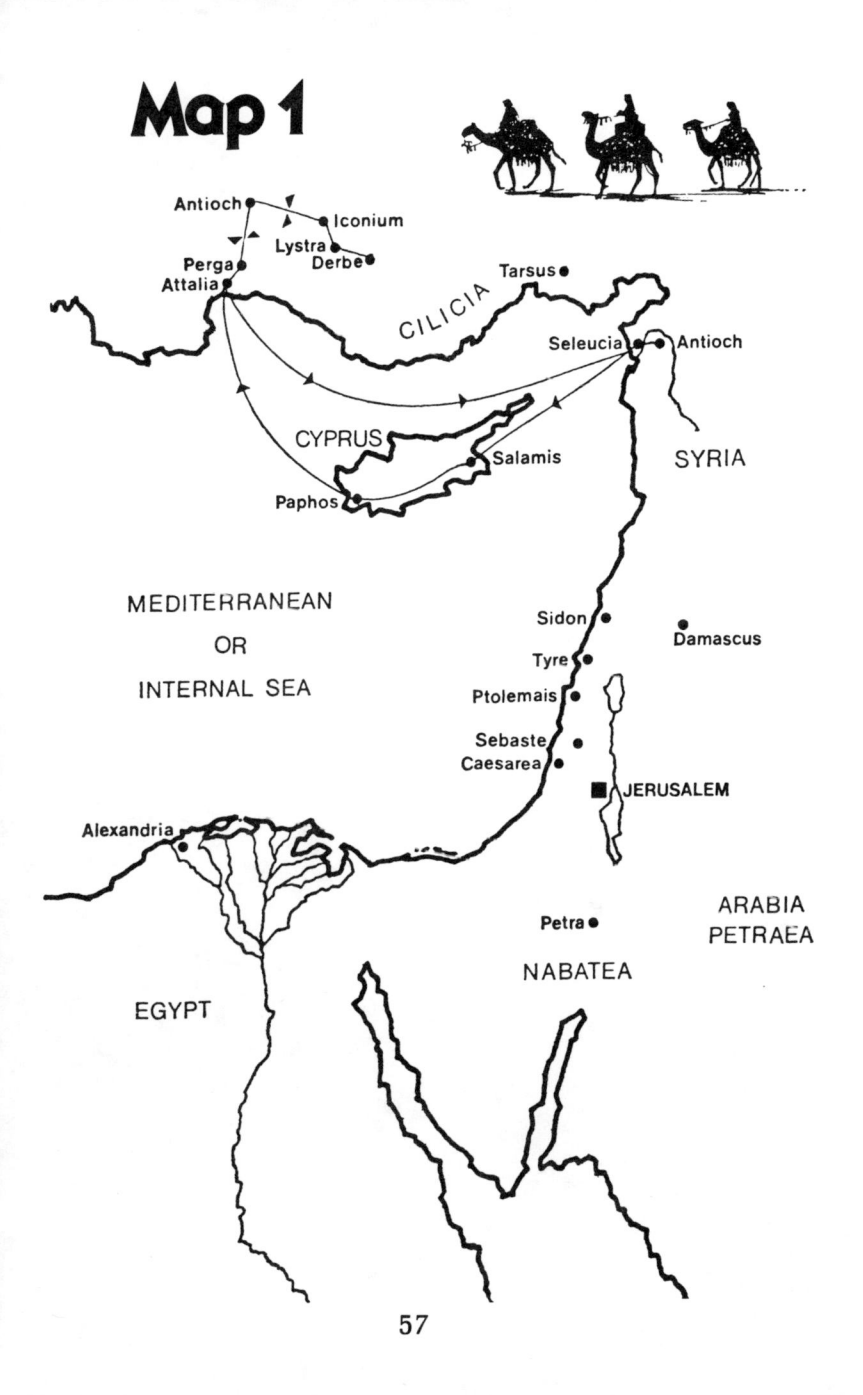

Map 2

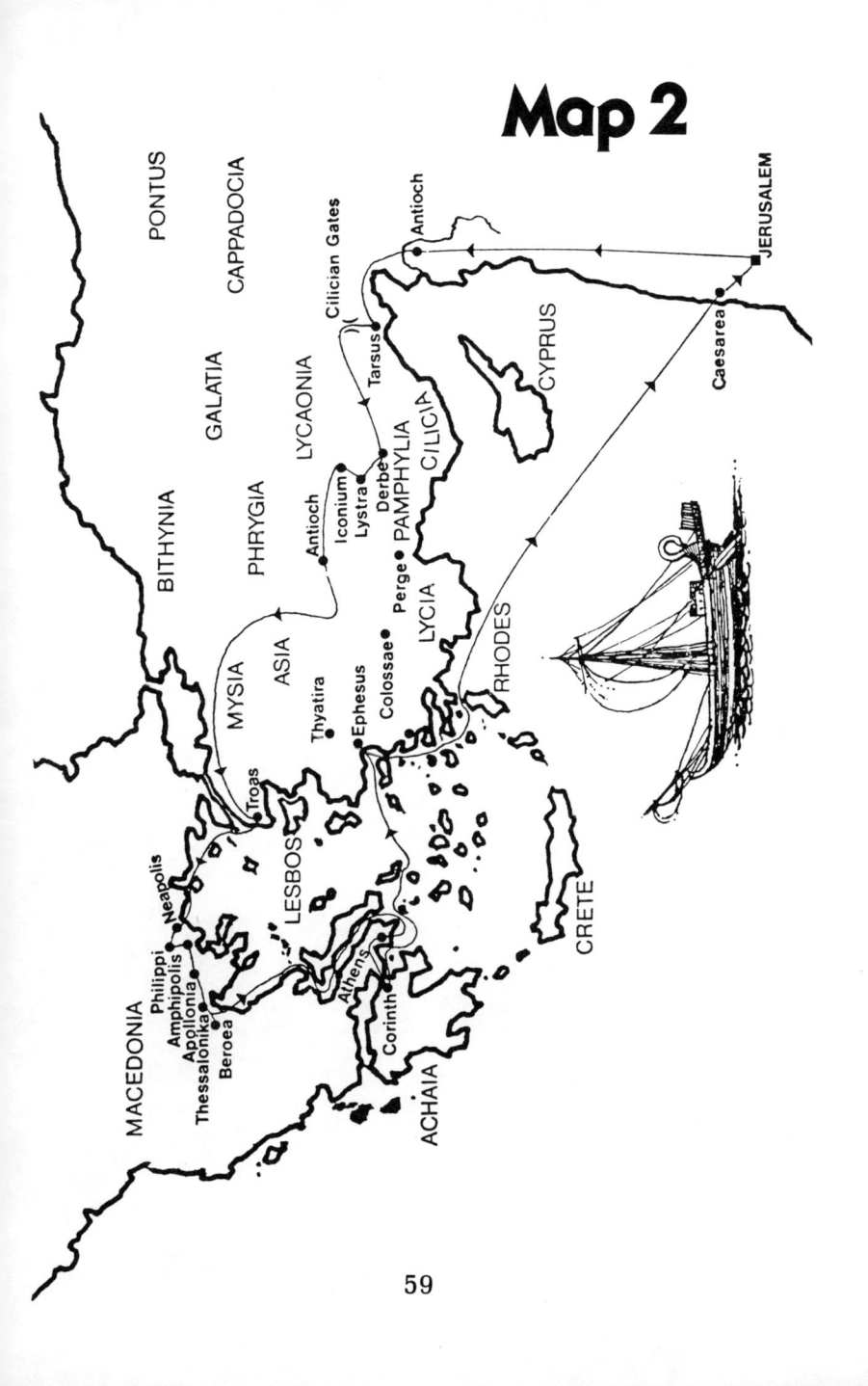

Map 3

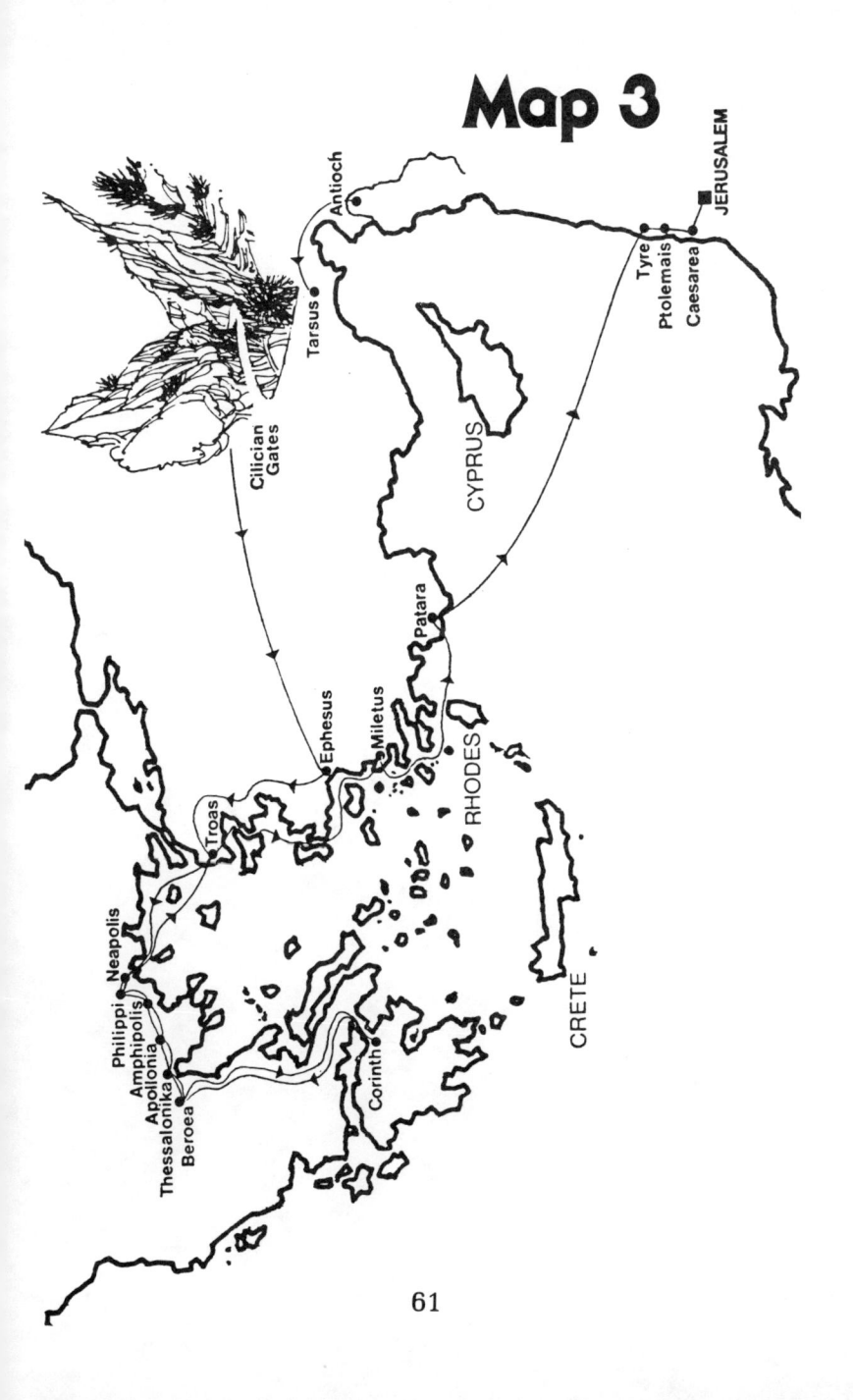

Map 4

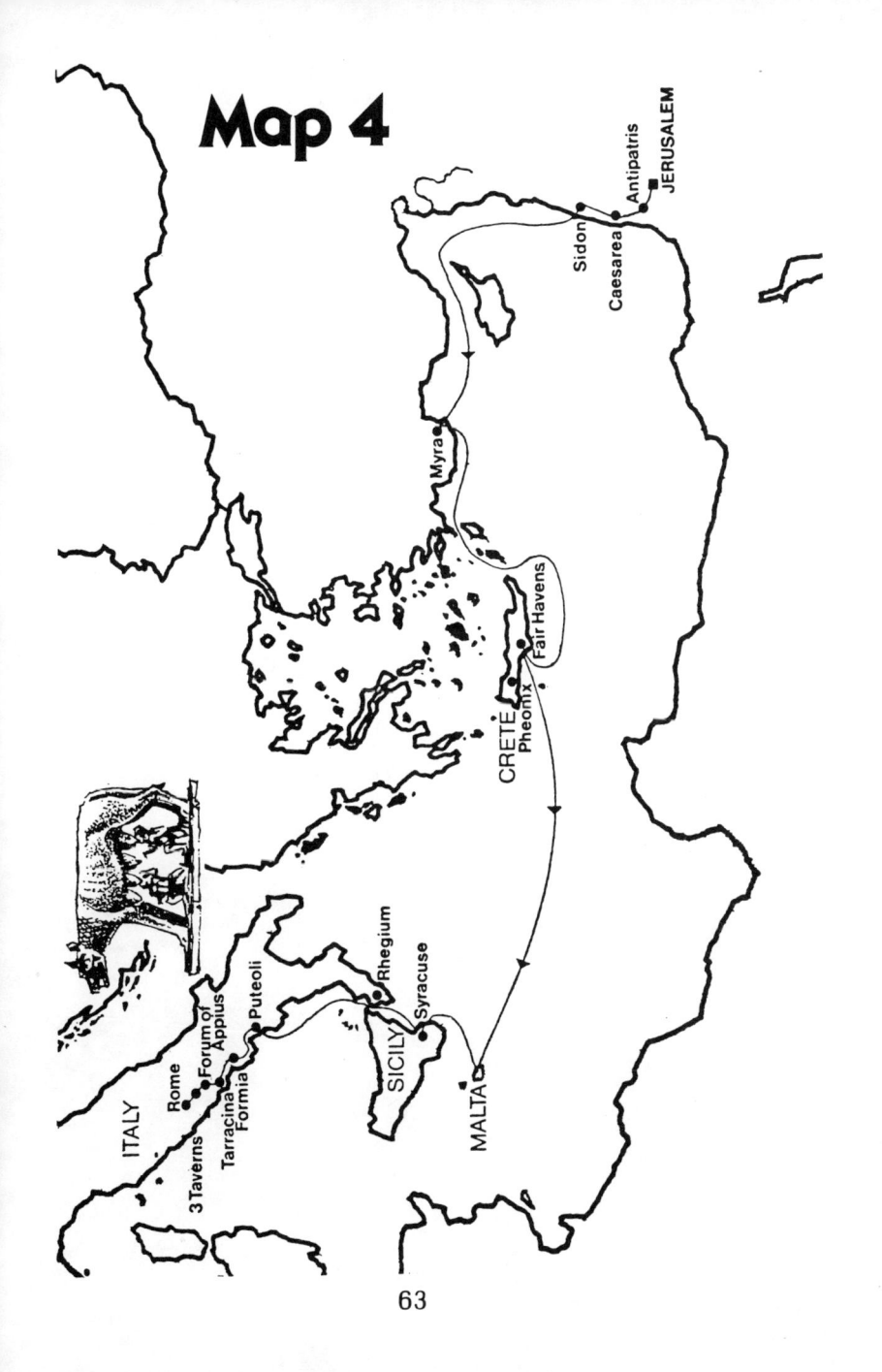